W9-AKB-464

Alexander Graham Bell

by Lola M. Schaefer

Consulting Editor: Gail Saunders-Smith, Ph.D.

Consultant: Judith Tulloch, Historian, Parks Canada,
Alexander Graham Bell National Historic Site

Pebble Books

an imprint of Capstone Press
Mankato, Minnesota

CHARLES CARROLL SCHOOL
LIBRARY

Pebble Books are published by Capstone Press
151 Good Counsel Drive, P.O. Box 669, Mankato, Minnesota 56002
http://www.capstone-press.com

© 2003 by Capstone Press. All rights reserved.
No part of this publication may be reproduced in whole or in part, or stored in a
retrieval system, or transmitted in any form or by any means, electronic, mechanical,
photocopying, recording, or otherwise, without written permission of the publisher.
For information regarding permission, write to Capstone Press,
151 Good Counsel Drive, P.O. Box 669, Dept. R, Mankato, Minnesota 56002.
Printed in the United States of America

1 2 3 4 5 6 08 07 06 05 04 03

Library of Congress Cataloging-in-Publication Data
Schaefer, Lola M., 1950–
    Alexander Graham Bell / by Lola M. Schaefer.
    p. cm.—(First biographies)
    Summary: Simple text and photographs introduce the life of Alexander
Graham Bell.
    Includes bibliographical references and index.
    ISBN 0-7368-1644-5 (hardcover)
    1. Bell, Alexander Graham, 1847–1922—Juvenile literature. 2. Inventors—
United States—Biography—Juvenile literature [1. Bell, Alexander Graham, 1897-1922.
2. Inventors.] I. Title. II. Series.
TK6143.B4 S35 2003
621.385′092—dc21
                                                                    2002011750

Note to Parents and Teachers

The First Biographies series supports national history standards for
units on people and culture. This book describes and illustrates the
life of Alexander Graham Bell. The photographs support early
readers in understanding the text. This book also introduces early
readers to subject-specific vocabulary words, which are defined
in the Words to Know section. Early readers may need assistance
to read some words and to use the Table of Contents, Words to
Know, Read More, Internet Sites, and Index/Word List sections of
the book.

Table of Contents

Family 5

Inventing 9

Inventing the Telephone 15

Words to Know 22

Read More 23

Internet Sites 23

Index/Word List 24

Time Line

1847
born

Alexander Graham Bell was born in Scotland in 1847. His father was a famous teacher who taught people how to speak well.

Scotland

Time Line

1847
born

Alexander's mother was deaf. She was still able to teach him to play the piano. Alexander was good at music and science.

the Bell family; Alexander is on the left.

Time Line

1847
born

Alexander was interested in sound. He also liked to invent things. He built a machine that could speak. He also tried to make his dog talk.

◀ Alexander using an early invention

Time Line

1847
born

1871
teaches deaf
students in Boston

In 1871, Alexander moved to Boston. During the day, he taught deaf students how to speak. At night, he did experiments with sound.

classroom at a school for the deaf

Time Line

1847
born

1871
teaches deaf
students in Boston

1874
begins work
with Tom Watson

12

Alexander wanted to learn more about electricity. In 1874, he met Tom Watson. Tom knew how electricity worked. They began to work together.

Electricity can make sound travel through wires.

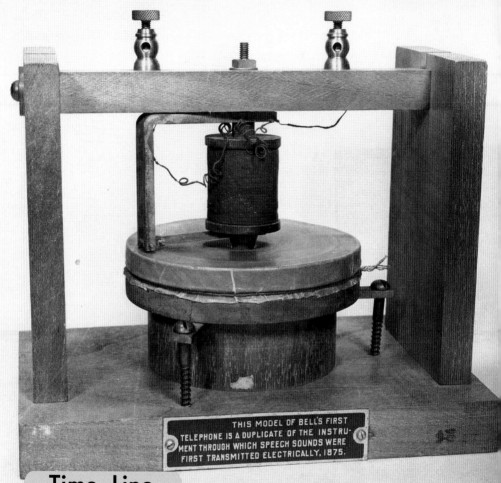

THIS MODEL OF BELL'S FIRST TELEPHONE IS A DUPLICATE OF THE INSTRUMENT THROUGH WHICH SPEECH SOUNDS WERE FIRST TRANSMITTED ELECTRICALLY, 1875.

Time Line

1847
born

1871
teaches deaf
students in Boston

1874
begins work
with Tom Watson

Alexander stopped teaching. He did experiments day and night. He and Tom wanted to invent a machine that could send voices from one place to another.

a model of Bell's first telephone

Time Line

1847
born

1871
teaches deaf
students in Boston

1874
begins work
with Tom Watson

On March 10, 1876, Alexander and Tom reached their goal. Alexander spoke to Tom through the first telephone.

◀ Alexander Graham Bell using his telephone

1876
invents telephone
with Tom Watson

Time Line

1847
born

1871
teaches deaf
students in Boston

1874
begins work
with Tom Watson

Alexander and Tom made the telephone better. Soon it could send voices many miles. In 1915, they made the first telephone call across the United States.

◄ the first telephone call across the United States

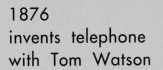

1876
invents telephone
with Tom Watson

1915
makes first telephone
call across the
United States

Time Line

1847
born

1871
teaches deaf
students in Boston

1874
begins work
with Tom Watson

Alexander spent his life inventing. He died in 1922. Alexander Graham Bell changed the way people communicate with one another.

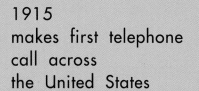

1876
invents telephone
with Tom Watson

1915
makes first telephone
call across
the United States

1922
dies

Words to Know

communicate—to share information, ideas, or feelings with another person by talking or writing

deaf—not able to hear any sounds, or only a very few sounds

electricity—a form of energy; electricity can be used to make sound waves pass through wires.

experiment—a test to try out an idea

famous—known to many people

goal—something that a person aims for

invent—to think up and make something new

machine—a piece of equipment made up of moving parts that is used to do a job

Read More

Gaines, Ann. *Alexander Graham Bell.* Discover the Life of an Inventor. Vero Beach, Fla.: Rourke Books, 2002.

Ross, Stewart. *Alexander Graham Bell.* Scientists Who Made History. Austin, Texas: Raintree Steck-Vaughn, 2001.

Shuter, Jane. *Alexander Graham Bell.* Lives and Times. Chicago: Heinemann Library, 2000.

Internet Sites

Track down many sites about Alexander Graham Bell. Visit the FACT HOUND at *http://www.facthound.com*

IT IS EASY! IT IS FUN!

1) Go to *http://www.facthound.com*

2) Type in: 0736816445

3) Click on "FETCH IT" and FACT HOUND will find several links hand-picked by our editors.

Relax and let our pal FACT HOUND do the research for you!

Index/Word List

born, 5
Boston, 11
built, 9
communicate, 21
deaf, 7, 11
died, 21
dog, 9
electricity, 13
experiments, 11, 15
famous, 5
father, 5

first, 17, 19
interested, 9
invent, 9, 15, 21
machine, 9, 15
mother, 7
moved, 11
music, 7
reached, 17
science, 7
Scotland, 5
send, 15, 19

sound, 9, 11
speak, 5, 9, 11
spoke, 17
students, 11
teacher, 5
telephone, 17, 19
United States, 19
voices, 15, 19
Watson, Tom, 13, 15, 17, 19

Word Count: 206
Early-Intervention Level: 18

Editorial Credits

Jennifer VanVoorst, editor; Heather Kindseth, cover designer and illustrator; Linda Clavel, illustrator; Juliette Peters, designer; Karrey Tweten, photo researcher

Photo Credits

A.G. Bell National Historic Site, 6
Corbis, 20; E. O. Hoppe', 4; Bettman, 8, 10, 14, 16; Charles E. Rotkin, 12
Getty Images/Hulton Archive, cover; Topical Press Agency, 1; Fox Photos, 18